LEARNING LOVE to JESUS…

His Precious Teachings

ARLENE ARENDS MAX
ILLUSTRATED BY WINDEL EBORLAS

ISBN: Softcover   978-1-5434-3262-6
       Hardcover   978-1-5434-3263-3
       EBook   978-1-5434-3264-0

*New King James Version (NKJV)
Scripture taken from the New King James Version®. Copyright © 1982 by Thomas Nelson. Used by permission. All rights reserved

*International Children's Bible (ICB)
The Holy Bible, International Children's Bible® Copyright© 1986, 1988, 1999, 2015 by Tommy Nelson™, a division of Thomas Nelson. Used by permission.

*Scripture quotations marked MSG are taken from THE MESSAGE. Copyright © 1993, 1994, 1995, 1996, 2000, 2001, 2002, 2003 by Eugene H. Peterson. Used by permission of NavPress Publishing Group. http://www.navpress.com/landing/bibles.aspx
Print information available on the last page

Rev. date: 08/01/2017

To order additional copies of this book, contact:
Xlibris
1-888-795-4274
www.Xlibris.com
Orders@Xlibris.com

HE TAUGHT US LOVE

Thank You, dear God, for the gift of Your son.
He taught us Your word and what must be done
To please You by doing the best that we can,
When He came down to earth and lived as a man.

His words live forever in Your holy book.
Great lessons are there, if we just take a look.
We'll learn how He loved all Your children the same,
And how He brought honor to Your holy name.

He taught us to put Your will first when we pray,
To forgive and serve others in a kind, humble way.
He taught us to give and He taught us to share.
He taught us to help and He taught us to care.

Now Father in heaven, almighty and great,
Please help us to learn from Your son while we wait
For that wonderful day when we meet You above.
We'll be thankful the lesson He taught us was LOVE!

NOT BY BREAD ALONE

After Jesus was baptized, He went all alone to pray
In the wilderness for forty days, with no food, by the way.
And then when He was starving, the devil came along,
And dared Him to turn stones into bread; that surely would be wrong.
He told the devil, "Man does not need bread to stay alive.
It is the word of God that people must have to survive."

The devil tried another trick that took them far away
To the temple in Jerusalem, and was bold enough to say,
"If You're God's son, jump off this peak. You won't get hurt at all,
Because God would never let His son be injured in a fall.
He promised to send angels to catch You in their hands."
But Jesus said, "Don't test the Lord. I do what God commands."

After that he took the Lord to a mountaintop so high
That they could see vast kingdoms, in this, his final try
To get the Lord to worship him and kneel down at his feet,
By promising Him those kingdoms, but that led to his defeat.
For Jesus said, "Get out of here! It's God I serve and praise."
The devil left, and angels came to serve Christ all His days.

(Matthew 4:1-11)

BLESSINGS

Blessings may not always be the things that we can see,
But God the Father gives us what is best for you and me.
Riches we don't have on earth, we'll have in heaven one day,
And even if we're sad and cry, He'll wipe our tears away.
Jesus promised all the humble ones, who want to do what's right,
That God will fill their lives with all that's perfect in His sight.
So if we're kind to others, helping with a heart that's pure,
We'll see God up in heaven, and our future will be sure.
He'll call us all His children, if we work at making peace.
And even if some hate us, God's love will just increase.
(Matthew 5:1-12)

LET YOUR LIGHT SHINE

God wants us all to shine as lights that light up every land,
Shining into life's dark corners, like a candle on a stand.
When we help folks as Jesus did, by bringing gifts of love,
We cheer the sad and lonely ones and honor God above.
So let's not hide our loving lights, but rather find a way
To spread God's love by doing good, and brightening someone's day.
(Matthew 5:14-16)

A NEW WAY

Jesus knew the ten commandments and taught God's laws were true,
But He showed the people what they meant
in ways that were quite new.
They knew the law said not to kill, but Jesus added more.
He said, "If you get angry, then you're breaking the same law!"
The people also knew to bring their gifts to God and pray,
But He explained, "If something's wrong,
leave your gift and walk away.
Find the person you have a problem with; talk it over, work it out.
Make peace…then go give God your gift."
That's a better way, no doubt.
(Matthew 5:21-24)

LOVE EVERYONE

The old way was to love your friend and hate your enemy.
But God loves good and bad alike, and Christ said so should we.
It isn't hard to love your friends, because they love you too.
Being kind to those who hate you is a harder thing to do.
Be good to them and pray for them, no matter what they say.
God's son loved everyone He met, a good example for us today.
(Matthew 5:43-48)

DO GOOD SECRETLY

Another lesson Jesus taught was how to help folks out.
He said to do good secretly and not to brag about
The things we do for others or the gifts that we may bring.
The praise of men means nothing, but our God sees everything.
In doing kind deeds quietly and humbly like our Lord,
We can be sure our loving God will give us our reward.
(Matthew 6:1-4)

PRAYING

Praying is our time to be alone with God each day,
To tell Him that we love Him with the simple words we say.
We close our eyes and fold our hands and say a quiet prayer.
Before we even speak one word, He knows our every care!
(Matthew 6:5-8)

THE LORD'S PRAYER

The Lord taught us to pray this way: first we praise God's holy name.
And as His will is done in heaven, say we want to do the same.
We ask Him for our daily food, and to forgive what we did wrong.
Ask for help forgiving others, and against evil to be strong.
For to God belongs the kingdom, where we one day want to be,
Since all power and all glory are with God eternally.
(Matthew 6:9-13)

TREASURES

Jesus taught us to be smart about the things we treasure.
So many things that we may have can bring us lots of pleasure.
But if we tie our hearts to them and they break or go away,
We'll be sad once they are gone, so He taught a better way.
He said that we should focus on God's treasures up above.
No one can ever ruin or steal our heavenly Father's love.
(Matthew 6:19-21)

LET'S NOT JUDGE

Jesus taught us not to judge, or call some people bad.
For if we do, then they might too, and that would make us sad.
Let's not be quick to judge our friends or tell them they are wrong.
Let's try to fix our own faults first, then help them to be strong.
(Matthew 7:1-5)

THE GOLDEN RULE

Another lesson from our Lord is called "The Golden Rule".
It tells us how we should behave at home, at play, at school.
Be sure to treat all people in a way that's kind and true.
In other words, in just the way you want them to treat you!
(Matthew 7:12)

GOD CARES FOR US

The Lord said not to worry about what to eat or wear.
Life is more than food and clothes. We're in our Father's care.
He gives the birds their food to eat, and He loves us even more.
He'll feed us as His children; of that you can be sure.
And look at all the flowers that bloom; they're dressed so beautifully!
He cares for everything He made. He'll give us what we need.
In everything remember to seek God's righteousness.
If we love God above all things, He'll give us what is best.
(Matthew 6:25-34)

MARY AND MARTHA

Once in a village where Jesus taught, two friends invited Him in.
Martha and Mary, her sister, were happy to welcome Him.
Martha got busy in the kitchen, making food for Him to eat,
While Mary listened to every word, as she sat down at His feet.
She wanted to hear what He would teach and not miss anything.
But Martha was serving and getting mad
that she was doing everything!
She came and said, "Lord, don't You care that she's not helping me?"
But Mary saw the important part that Martha could not see.
For Jesus answered, "Martha, you're working much too hard,
And you're missing what really matters. Mary chose the better part."
(Luke 10:38-42)

THE DOCTOR

Jesus ate with sinners, which some folks thought was bad.

They didn't understand His ways and the loving heart He had.

They thought He should be with them, since they knew all God's laws,

Not waste His time with cheaters, but His answer made them pause.

He said, "Why should a doctor go to those folks who are well?

He helps the sick! Now stop and think, and see if you can tell

Why I am here with sinners, who need mercy more than you."

He wanted all to feel God's love and find forgiveness too.

(Matthew 9:10-13)

THE SIMPLE ONES

The Lord Jesus thanked His Father that He hid things from the wise,

And showed the truth to simple ones with open hearts and eyes.

For only those who listen and learn from Him are blest.

He promised He would help them and give the weary ones rest.

(Matthew 11:25-30)

WHO ARE MY BROTHERS?

When Jesus was told His mother and His brothers were at the door,

He taught the people something they had never heard before.

He asked, "Who are My brothers? Not just My family dear,

But all who do My Father's will...like My disciples here."

(Matthew 12:46-50)

LET THEM COME TO ME

Many people came to listen when Jesus was in town.
The mothers brought their children, and even set them down
Right where the Lord was teaching, for they heard that He was kind.
He always spoke so lovingly, they thought He wouldn't mind.
They wanted Him to pray with them, to bless each little one.
But His disciples stopped them, saying "This should not be done!"
Our loving Lord corrected them, "Let the children come to Me.
God's kingdom will belong to those who are just like them, you see."
(Matthew 19:13-15)

PRECIOUS CHILDREN

All the children liked to come to Jesus for they knew
He loved them just the way they are, with hearts so pure and true.
When His disciples asked Him who the greatest in heaven would be,
He showed them all a little child and said, "Look, and you will see
That if you can be humble like this precious little one,
Then you will have all that you need the greatest to become.
In fact, whoever will accept such a child in My name,
With a pure, believing heart, accepts Me just the same."
(Matthew 18:1-5)

THE RICH YOUNG MAN

A rich young man came to the Lord and asked what he should do
To make sure he would go to heaven, when his life was through.
So Jesus told this man to keep the laws of God each day,
Not to lie and not to steal or hurt others in any way.
He told the Lord that he had kept those laws and all the rest,
But then he asked, "Must I do more to be forever blest?"
So Jesus said, "Sell all you have; give the money to the poor.
Do that, and then come follow Me. Heaven's treasures will be yours."
(Matthew 19:16-21)

FORGIVE AGAIN

Christ taught that forgiveness matters, on earth and up in heaven.
So Peter asked, "Must I still forgive if my brother's sins total seven?"
"Seven times won't be enough," our dear Lord answered him.
"Forgive him several hundred times, and then forgive again."
(Matthew 18:21-22)

THE QUESTION

A smart and clever lawyer once tried to trick God's son,
By asking which commandment was the most important one.
Jesus said that it would be, "Love God with all your heart,
And also love your neighbor, for that's the second part."
(Matthew 22:35-40)

GOD SO LOVED THE WORLD

In this most precious lesson, Jesus told us why He came.
It was to save all people who believe in His holy name.
He said, "God loved the world so much, He gave His only son."
He taught us that eternal life can be for everyone.
(John 3:16)

LOVE EACH OTHER

When Jesus knew the time had come to return to God above,
He prayed for all His followers and assured them of His love.
He told them, "Love each other, in the way that I love you.
All will know you're My disciples by the loving things you do."
(John 13:34-35)

PROVE YOUR LOVE

Our Savior made it very clear that He and His Father are one.
We show we love the Father, by loving Christ His son.
He said, "Do all I've taught you, and you'll prove your love for Me.
Then God will show He loves you too, throughout eternity."
(John 14:19-21)

Printed in the United States
By Bookmasters